HEAD!

Written and illustrated
by PriceyPoet.

For you,

Thank you.

CONTENTS

Prologue

Right in the centre of a temper,
or when the thought is on the tip of my tongue,
in between the words that are easily found,
sits the rhythm in which I write.

As a poet my aim is to write about topics that are hard
to summarise. The thoughts you get that don't seem to
be able to be submerged into sentences.

The moments that leave you speechless are the ones
I'm interested in most.

As a pre-pandemic performance poet, most of the
pieces in this collection were originally written to be
performed live for an audience.
Any one of the poems in this selection, started off as a
singular phrase that sat in my mind in a particular
rhythm that was then built on bit by bit,
beat by beat,
until it seemed finished.

'Art is never finished, only abandoned.'
(Leonardo DaVinci, among others)

This collection of personal poetry is an urge to society to talk about how they're feeling.

Be it through discussion with others, or expressing yourself through art and poetry, I believe it is vital for humans to at least attempt to express those thoughts that escape words.

The topics that polite conversation dodges around, are plainly found here.

HOW AM I?

(THE QUESTION)

My fists clench and my stomach wrenches.
Every time I think of all the shit
that is too hard to mention.
I want to say whats going on inside
but my minds eyes is going blind.
My fists clench and my stomach wrenches.
Every time I think of all the shit
I just don't want to mention.
You want to know whats going on inside
but my minds eye is going blind-

How am I?

Fine.
I'm fine.
Honest, I'm fine.
Yeah, alright.
A little tired.
Had a long night.

But yeah,
I'm fine.

That was a lie.
A big old pork pie.
A line I've tried a thousand times, to nearly eve
friend of mine, so to reach the truth beneath the lie, you
have to read between the lines.

I'm fine.

It's a way of getting my mind-sight, out of the limelight.
Even if the times right, your line of questioning is likely
to make me dizzy like we're at a blind height,
and leave the conversation aimless like
the three blind mice.

When I'm asked the question theres no telling what I
might do,
and it takes hindsight to,
recognise that maybe I should not have tried that move
when you asked me to
open up and tell you the truth.

But in my experience, that situation can lead to
complication,
it takes great articulation on both parts

for it to be a conversation of both hearts.
Its far too easy to let superficial issues rear their ugly head.
Don't let your super ego dictate whats said.

Just answer honest. Listen honest too.
Never try and tell them what you would do,
unless you've stepped foot into a pair of their shoes.
Now you know what you need to do the next time you ask someone,
How are you?

TIDE

I don't want to die.

But, I stand and look at the tracks as the eastbound approaches.
Its seemingly so slow, it'd be so easy, wouldn't take much to go.
I only ever do this when I'm alone.

I love my life.

Yet, I stop over bridges and hear the call. The simplicity of it all.
Not a fight or a brawly
Just a flight,
then a fall.

I'm happy.

And,
I held a knife to my neck just to see how hard it'd be,
but immediately recognised this was not for me.

I don't want to bleed.

Too much a horrible scene.
Too much mess to clean.

This isn't a poem about suicide.
Just a tannoy that these thoughts tend to tip toe through
the tide.
Apparently there's a bigger picture that I'm yet to find.
It's easy to get lost in your thoughts
when you're losing your mind.

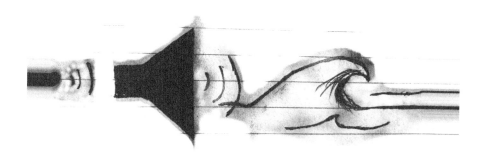

BOYS BIRDS BOUNCERS

Boys birds and bouncers busy bumbling about.
Musics proper shit speakers way too loud,
If you want a drink you're gonna have to shout,
And you'll lose half your mates with the size of this
crowd.

These lads getting randy these lads squaring up
Why is it always the same mate who ends up fucked?

Who's taking him home? Its not me
Just stick him in the backseat of a random taxi
See, girls got glamour, well some do anyway.
Walk straight in girls sorry lads not today

"Oi you! Back of the queue.

IDs out please, you're not eighteen "

Friday night rush, spent dole and wages
Act like animas released from their cages
Smart shoes and shirt dress code is key
And if someones being mouthy
You just charge them double entry.

On this door night after night,
People so pissed don't know left from their right
'cause all of life gets chucked here and theres not a
better sight
Than a sticky floor packed on a Friday night.

Come one, come all. The more the merrier,
As the night draws to a close you're head'll get heavier,
Barely see straight never mind walking,
You met a nice girl and you got to talking

Part of you was thinking that this could be it,
But you wake up in the morning and you don't know
who she is.

You'll have a banging headache and stomach will hurt,
Come Monday morning when you're straight back to
work.
Piecing together memories with all your friends

Then you work

Work

Work

Work

Work

Just to do it again.

ETERNITY

What does eternity look like?
I imagine placing a stone on a field of gold.

Then another, and another, and another,
and another…

Keep placing them down until they're a stretched out
before you further than the eye can see.
Until the line you have drawn in stone on sand, is
touching the moon and sun on each horizon.

You're stood in the middle of forever.

Can you see it?

You're still not close.

I want eternity.

Real eternity.
I want space and time to scribble out the entire works
of Shakespeare before breakfast.

I want to hang for hours, dance for days, work for weeks, meditate for months, yearn for years for the feeling humanity cling to only in death.

We are told no one can live forever, yet promised eternal life.

If eternity comes after death, then what is it that we call life?

We should cry at christenings. Dance for deceased at their funerals.

The minute that we're born we are condemned to die. The second we are confronted with death, we are set free to live.

Supposedly.

You can keep your eternity earned only through death. I want to be alive to experience my forever.

What does eternity look like?

An animated ever changing watercolour of a tropical landscape?

Or is it staring at your own self-portrait?

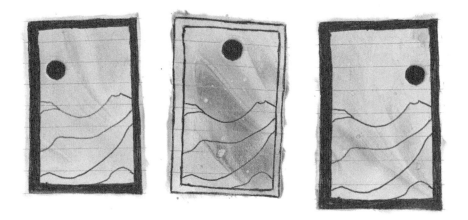

A SENSE OF PRIVILEGE

I wanted to write another poem about race,
because all the others I've written seem to sound like
silence.
When Colin took a knee the world knelt on his neck,
so you should start to expect the fire and violence.

See, I understand,
everyones life can seem a sort of a struggle
but the power privilege possesses,
can make you forget amongst the muddle,
like jumping in a puddle
we don't care who else gets wet.

My white privilege looks like this;
I've only been handcuffed and detained once.
As soon as it was over I called the officer a cunt.
I walked along my way.
Got on with my day.
And was never once concerned about getting beaten
up.

My white privilege sounds like the kid who got on
stage, with Dave, at Glastonbury,
I admit at the time I thought it was kind of heavy,
but the media wrote his name like he was the next big
thing,
due to the pigment of his skin.
This kid was no rapper, surely they could tell this?
Just a White boy in front of a Black artist, like Elvis.

My white privilege feels like this;
The bouncers shake my hand and tell me have a good
night.
The club is never full and they never want to fight.
And I never feel them pat me down,
even if my jaw is swinging round.
'cause they know I'm no trouble and they know that
'cause I'm white.

My white privilege smells like the loose grass in my
bag that is stinking out the train.
Commuters trying to work who it is but no one looks
my way,
and I'm not feeling any fear,
when that copper's getting near,
'cause we both know that, for a fact,
he'll find someone else to blame.

My white privilege tastes like this;
A proper big bitter pill of ibuprofen,
thats heavy hard to swallow.
Having to acknowledge the past before moving to
tomorrow.
We might not like the taste, but it must trump hate,

and is surely better than drowning in your sorrow.

Real change comes from fixing fundamental flaws,
whether they've been etched into your being, or
carved into your laws,
I'm only telling you what my privilege looks like so you
might recognise yours.

FACE/TIME

I was on FaceTime/to a great mate of mine/when I discovered all it needs is for you to take the time/look into your mates eyes/and you might realise/theres sadness in their eyes.
'cause even from the pixelated image on my screen/it was clear to me/that there was something wrong with him which means theres something wrong with me.
Thats called empathy/not apathy/but thats just me/ I seem to radically/ and tragically/ choose between/ two extremes.

So I asked my pal what was going on/ he said "nah nothing" I said don't get me wrong/
Im not saying your a liar or you're not being real/ I'm just saying that we're allowed to chat about how we feel/and I'm not trying to turn this into a big deal/but it seems obvious you're trying to conceal how you feel.

Shrugged it off didn't want to discuss it/ don't know if its embarrassment or if he just hates fussing/so went on for a little bit, avoiding the topic/ when I remembered a statistic that I thought could stop this.

I said bruv; 84 men kill themselves a week/in this country/hows that for a news leak/ sad that the truths so peak/even sadder that these lads would rather take their lives than be deemed weak/ toxic masculinity/ letting negativity/ take up most of the vicinity/ instead of positivity/ that could spread across infinity/ and end up restoring whats left of your sanity/He just sat with me.

With these words my brother, my pal, my friend, he let himself begin/
 to really let me in/sat there and told me what caused his head to spin.
I'm not gonna divulge what he told me/'cause I believe that was for my ears only.

but what I can tell you is; we had a session/on depression.
we held a piety/ to anxiety.
we took these topics and left no stone unturned/
so many lessons learned/
Took the mechanism of our minds apart,
 found out exactly what made these cogs turn/built a fire let it burn.
Threw all our worries and stresses into the inferno,
 watched them go up in flames/I was amazed/
At the blaze/that we created/ and I knew if we had all day/
 I could have stayed/at this for ages/ 'cause one conversation/
is wort a thousand pages/ so listen as I say this/

I hung up sat back and my head was light/
as it turns out not every chat has to be a fight/
and forcing myself to hide/
meant I wound myself tight/but one conversation turned my fright/
 to delight.

Im not saying that convos are cures/
or putting up a front like my depression is no more.
when it gets rough for you remember what I told you/
restores confidence and strength and has you moving
bolder.

The bad but beautiful truth is it can be hard as fuck.
put it in your own hands/you've no chance/ if you leave
it down to luck.
 grab a friend or a loved one mash it out with your
mate/
keep a firm grip on the reality of your mind state/
tell them everything you think and feel leave nothing
unsaid/
Its a long and bumpy ride guys so please/
Mind your heads.

HURRICANE KISSES

Hurricane kisses.

on a day that was hotter than the rest.

Smiles.

sweat drips   down   the chest,

as she lights   a cigarette.

Pick pockets roam   the streets of London

looking for   star   crossed   lovers.

Whose stares   are   scarcely broken,

a multitude of colours.

Green stains   on a white shirt,

muddy bums and lemonade,

the Thames looks blue today.

Don't leave your phone on the table.

even when you think it's sound.

Don't leave your drink unattended,

especially with those lads around.

Let's get out of here she said,

there's too much noise in my head.

She said;

can you just hold me?

he said

yes.

SOCIAL

BUTTERFLY

I was never one to consider myself a social butterfly.
More like a fly on the wall than the belle of the ball.
More akin to a bumble bee buzzing by,
ignoring the laws and force by which we have to abide.
Taking no notice of the scientists advice, the rumour
and lies -
flapping its wings and choosing to fly.

And much like the humble bumble bee, people tend to
treat me with caution afraid of the sting I can stick in
without warning. unaware of the fact that my sting is
kept back for when I'm attacked.

There is nothing to fear the of the bumble bee.
Just stay out of its face,
Leave it some space,
To pollinate.

I was never one to consider myself a social butterfly.
More like the very hungry caterpillar.
Wouldn't find me throwing shapes in disarray at a
wedding or birthday-
Would find me, fixing a plate, to stuff in my face, at the
buffet.
'cause like the hungry caterpillar, I'm more of a stay-at-
home-and-chiller.

Full of hope and vigour, but this earthly form, tends to
store, energy for a rainy day.

Now it never seems to stop raining.

So it seems each and every day, the energy I saved, is
dripping till its drained, faintly fading away, now
nothing remains.

I was never one to consider myself a social butterfly.
But I swear the walls of this concrete cocoon are way
too strong
When we finally emerge I'm putting my best shoes on,
Matter of fact, better than that, ill put a new suit on,
Blare the speakers up full blast nothing but good tunes
on,
Taking every chance I ever get to sing you songs.
Linking up with every person who's said 'its been too
long'
'cause it has been too long,
no I'm still not done.

Im hanging with all my pals for what will feel like
eternity
Im going home see my family, till mumzy is sick of me
Kicking balls in the park till I fuck my dodgy knee
Singing on the tube like nobody's watching me.
Nobody's stopping me.

I can say it with certainty -
all this time at home, on my own,
wasn't helping but hurting me.

Although it's late, just wait for soon,
We will kick out way out of this cocoon,
The sun will shine, no rain in the sky,
And I will try, to be somewhat a social butterfly.

SCRAPS

Lads dad said never hit a soul, unless the hit you first,
So his first scrap started with those words.
Come on hit me then, repeated like a verse
Till he can cause this kid to crack and break his nerve.

He threw the first punch but only cause lad made him
Then theres fists flying, shitheads shouting, manic
mayhem.

Only stops when sir come through and gripped his
ripped shirt
Chucked him to his office and went fkin berserk,
Said 'Lad what you trying to do? Throw all this work?"
Lad sat silent, the emptiness of words.

Then he makes the phone call,
Seems like seconds mum arrives.
He's thrown into the car he slouches down by her side.
She says she's disappointed, He says he's not
surprised.
Then they sit in total silence for the rest of the ride.

"Go to your room, Lad. You just wait till dad gets home."
He tells her gladly, she says 'smartass leave your phone.'

He's sat in his doom, dads car pulls up the drive.
Hears the door slam as he steps inside.
He hears some shouted whispers, then a yell of don't you care.
hears his heavy hoof steps as they climb up the stairs.

At this point Lad is shitting bricks.
He's thinking that this could be it,
So he starts to grab his rucksack,
and filling it with all his shit.

Door opens.   Hi.   Alright.
"What's this I've heard about you having a fight?"
Lad starts to spout the story but before he can begin,
The big man interrupts him with-
"okay but did you win?"

Wasn't expecting a question.
More like a sentence.
He said what about detention?
But lad gets more work done in there than lessons.

That was pretty much it. No shouting. No fighting.
Just came up to see/if his son had faced defeat.

Lad has carried this with him. It seems so sewed into his seams.
Hard to unteach a lesson that got you through your teens.
Alive and in one piece.

Now when he's sober he's calm.
But I think, drink, links you to your past,

And gets you doing a lot less good than harm.

So this is his apology for the lessons that were taught to
he,
He's swimming hard but honestly some times he finds it
hard to breathe.
So sorry, sorry for every black eye, nose bleed, shit
night out, twisted ankle, argument,
headache or tear I've ever caused anybody. Including
me.

Love Your Neighbour as Yourself

"Love your neighbour as yourself" - Mark 12:31

As a man without religion I thought I'd finally found the
one

So I asked from which holy book? The Torah? The
Quran?

A voice replied "Yes... But read this one if you can"

As I was handed down a bible I swear my life was
changed

as I endeavoured to read every letter, of every word on
every page

It started off so sweet, with a couple named Adam and
Eve

But as the book went on I read some things I couldn't
believe.

A book full of contradictions, between the old and the
new,

I jotted down a few, so I could pass them on to you.

Love your neighbour as yourself, unless of course they are gay,

for that's an "abomination", and something he won't tolerate

Love your neighbour as yourself, unless of course they are Jews,

Muslim, Sikh, Buddhist, or even Hindu

For these should all be converted, or killed and not sent to heaven,

and yes it really says that: Deuteronomy 17:7.

This book also began to spout a lot of racial hatred

which got me wondering where this religion was created.

Found out that in the start the book was in a different language,

and has been battled against and for causing untold anguish

I'm talking mercilessly killing those who DONT BELIEVE

and mercilessly sacrificing those who DO BELIEVE

thinking of all the bloodshed makes it difficult to conceive,

I preferred it at the start with that Adam and that eve

Love your neighbour as yourself, seems a tad ironic now,

I think I'll choose a new religion, what's that one... with
the cows?
There are also so many things followers of this book
choose to ignore
like the fact your most definitely not supposed to eat
pork,
or shave your beard, cut your hair, drink wine in
church
but something's I read were the worst of the worst.
If a woman is raped, she must marry her rapist,
this brought me to the conclusion that God is a Sadist.

Love your neighbour as yourself, something I do
believe
and there are many things in this book with which I am
inclined to agree
but its just that half the things in there don't seem to
compute,
maybe its time for out with the old and in with the new,
testaments that is, 'cause I've just got to say
Religion is not like a wine; it doesn't get better with
age.

Now its fine to say that "things have changed now"
but i still can't quite really understand how
You can build a religion around these words,
then forget them down the line,

just because you, so desperately want to change with
the times,
keep your popularity up so people still donate the
funds,
without ever really questioning where this all came
from.
people are so willing to ignore the shit in this book
and if you go to church but haven't read it then you
need to take a look.
'cause spirituality is one thing, religion is another
I won't pray to your God, but i'll still call you my
brother

Reading this book caused much confliction,
but I do understand how its such an addiction
its not just through routine, or the fear of growing old
its something much deeper and it comes from the soul
People want to be told what's right, and what's wrong,
so they gather in a building pray prayers, and sing
songs,
but I'm certain we already know what's wrong and
what's right,
you'll find morality with in, so stop looking at the skies.

DREAMS HATE ME

The woman of my dreams - hates me.
Though she would never say,
but it seems its clear as day,
she really hates the way,
I always am.

And I can't fault her.
Though I may never falter,
I'm stubborn as blood stain,
stuck on a school shirt.

I'm loud and quick to anger,
spew bile in the face of love.
I don't see how she sees any handsome features,
in my soggy soul.

I'm a horrible child.
That's always been easy for me to say,
though you'd never hear her mutter,
any of the same.

There's more hope in her finger,
than lingers in my figure.
And more despair in my body hair,
than she has in her head.

I get lost in my rage,
That's hard for me to say,
The only route I see out,
Is lit up by her face.

I'm sorry, I'm always sorry,
For being always wrong.
I can't express my feelings,
Unless they are through song.

And I'm sorry it's a cop out.

I'm sorry for making it easy,
To hate me or to leave me.
But please if you can believe me,
I'm really trying to fix me.

I know I've lots of work to do,
I shouldn't take things out on you,
You've always been the best of you,
And I've always been just alright.

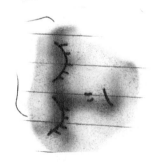

INTEGRITY

The British Broadcasting company.
Seems like they've got the wrong end of the stick to me.
I was watching the news last week, and they said that
JC had too much integrity.
Not JC from the biblical tense, I'm taking of the man
who's trying to bring political sense,
to this for gone era, the press say his talk is foggy, but
I've never been able to see it clearer.
While some are trying their best to kick peace away,
he's the only one trying to bring it nearer.
And yet they say he's a man burdened by his integrity.
A common insult to the left, but how can a man have too
much of a thing I can only hope to possess?
Integrity: adherence to moral and ethical principles.
Integrity: the state of being whole, entire, or
undiminished.
Integrity: a sound, unimpaired, or perfect condition.
Three definitions.
Not one gives answer, to how they use it as slander.
Well I'm all for a man with integrity, next to a party
who's only worry is plausible deniability.

So when this Titanic hits ice they can jump ship, and I'm
gonna be with the man helping the mothers and the
small kids.
to stay afloat, not give up hope 'cause he's the leader
we'd all need if none of us could vote.
He was the type of kid who'd find a bird with a broken
wing, nurse it back to health, even listen to it sing.
Whereas Boris and his boys, could find the same bird,
find out it was disabled and kick it to the curb.

But yeah, you could say he's too soft. Because he has a
moral code.
And when he says he's hungry, he's hungry for change,
not just hungry for your vote.
hungry for fairness, not just hungry for your notes.
And he wont push a button, that'll cause a whole nation
to explode.
Yet these words are dished out like insults,
Followers made out to be part of some mad cult,
We're all Liberal Demons, condemning religion,
When in reality they're just afraid of anything different.

Integrity. Seems to me to be what this country needs.
Instead of people who's only worry is if they can claim
it on their fees.
Yet the BBC, put messages on my screen, telling me
these aren't the things a leader should be.

Don't let the media warp your view of these words.
Integrity, honesty, loyalty. You need to know their
worth.
These are the things i was taught to strive for from
birth.
So to put a negative spin on them is simply absurd.
But they'll do it, to push their agenda, push their
beliefs.
Put their wants, over other peoples needs.
'cause thats just the nature of the selfish beast,
and thats just the way its always been,
so if you want change i guess you'll need,
one small thing,
Integrity.

SHE WRITES

Theres a girl I can see,
writing notes like me,
wonder what it could be,
she's jotting down neatly,
while my pen slashes and flicks like a storm,
in my notebook thats old and worn,
crooked and torn.

Hers so neat,
words find their feet,
perfect sitting right on the line,
I rush through she takes her time,
Wonder what story spills from her pen,
looks up clocks me look at her again,
then shoots me a smile almost like she knows
what my pen is telling before the words start to flow
Hand picks up pace, she's stuck on a thought,
chewing on her pencil I've seen this before,
she's not quite sure,
what word comes next,
looks out again and takes a big breath,
lets the word come to her, lets out sigh,

takes off her glasses to adjust her eyes,
fiddles for a pen she's tryna find,
picks it up and continues to write.

She's got things in her ears to deafen out sound,
cant let the noise around block out what she's writing
down,
must be loud in her head, and I now how that feels,
just 'cause its in your head, doesn't mean its not real.
What is it that she writes, just let me see,
literature, lyrics, essay or poetry,
whatever it is will remain hidden from me,
for all I know she's jotting down a list of he groceries.

She writes and her pen simmers down to a halt,
lifts up her book locks it shut like a bolt.
see the page is done for now
nothing else to write down,
she starts to gather her things get up from the ground,
she has a look back to check she's left nothing behind,
am I invisible or is she blind,
'cause she can look but
he sure wont find,
the impression that she's left on my mind.

Id let her autograph my headstone,
id let her scribble on my skin

Id let her doodle on my best clothes,
and she can use permanent ink.

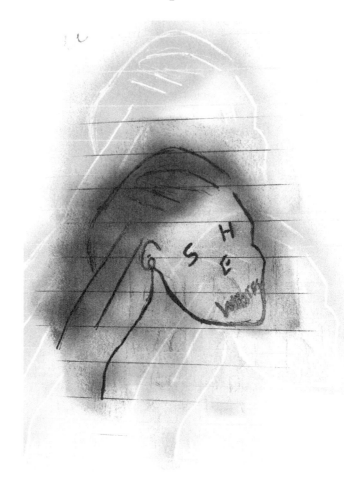

HAPPINESS

If you see happiness,
tell her where I am.
'cause I've been really craving,
for her to hold my hand.

If you see hatred,
send him the other way,
he's doing my fucking head in man,
he's bugging on my brain.

I was seeing jealousy,
she was sitting next to me,
I opened my eyes to see,
it was my anxiety.

If you see love,
please do me a favour,
tell her that she's beautiful,
I never got to say to her.

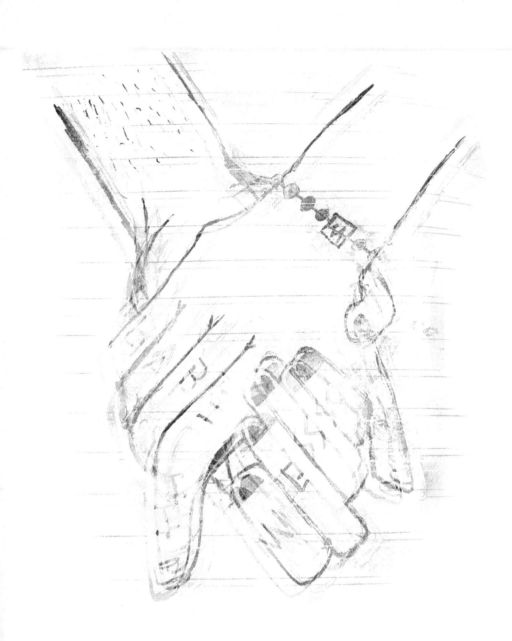

INSIDE OUT

I sat down and tried to cry but there was no tears

coming out,

so I swift picked up my pen and had a little shout,

see thats the only way I get what's inside, out,

otherwise, I'm always left feeling, inside out.

I've tried reading books, but its really hard to focus,

you know I used to like sports but don't as I get older.

I swear that I've aged twenty years inside a week

and yes I've seen my future and yes I know its bleak.

Somebody please tell the others to leave me alone,

but every time they do sadness belling up my phone.

I cant flip the off switch to social isolation,

'cause every time I do I end up hanging with my

hatred.

A homeless man stopped me asked me for a cigarette,

as I obliged I clocked and listened to what he said,

he said "sorry bro, could I nick a cigarette".

Im sorry to disappoint you poets but thats all he fucking

said.

CHIPPY LANE

I found God once,

he was drunk on Chippy Lane.

It was four in the morning,

he was bleeding from his brain.

He had just been killing time,

turning water into wine,

when the silly sod went and chatted up Johno's wife.

He tried to apologise,

offered all the blokes some wine,

then one of Johno's pals came and smacked Christ

from behind.

His head smacked back, crashed on the pavement.

Police, paramedics everybody making way for them.

Copper tried to stop me, asked me for s statement,

when God pointed me out and was like 'Theres

something I need to say to him'.

I was like, is that you? Are you God?

He was like "shutup man, obviously not.

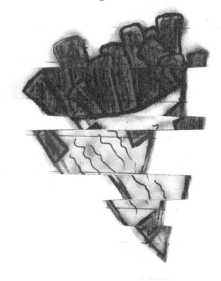

PERMANENT INK

I'd let her autograph my headstone.

I'd let her scribble on my skin.

I'd let her doodle on my best clothes.

And, she can use permanent ink.

HOW AM I?

(the answer)

How am I?

My head hurts daily stomach knots but the hour,
my palms sweat constantly, I'm a total coward.
I hide from how I feel until i reach my room,
where I can let it out through screams of doom.
Muffle by a pillow pressed against my lips,
so the world around cant hear the sound of my mind
when it dips,
into one of its low down states, from which theres no
escape.
If I tell somebody, they just ask me if I'd ate,
as if my mind couldn't conjure these demons on a full
belly,
or they recommend something to watch on the telly,
to distract me from the scheduled programming of my
mind,

I can only barricade these thoughts for some time.

Told someone, sometimes, suicide sits in my mind.
Don't know if it registered of if they were just blind,
to what that would mean if I had the gall to see it
through,
she nonchalantly shrugged it off let conversation
continue.

People tell me to talk, but never tell them to listen,
thoughts like Guy Fawkes, not very well hidden.
My heads a cave.
Only one way to escape.
I see light, hope, its day.
Not the sight, of that, which lays.
At the end of the route, that only the unlucky follow
through.

Are they unlucky? Unfortunate? unfulfilled?
Or were there other factors that cause the milk to spill.
Is it all down to the place and time?
They couldn't see another end to the line.
No other option, than to use a full stop.
When using a semi-colon just might increase the odds;
Of the spirits soldier on in the fleshy imperfect vessel,
I've heard all it takes is a chat, and a kettle.

Speak hope in your home, message mates for a brew,
Listen to them when they try and talk to you.

Or, if you'd like, you can pour yourself a pint,
do whatever it takes to get them to spill their mind.

How are you?
I hope I didn't bring down the mood,
I promise thats not what I'm trying to do,
its just what tends to happen when you write with truth.
Usually i'm quite a quiet guy, strong and silent type,
but you cant assume that shyness is the reason for my
silence,
its just that when I shut my eyelids I'm reminded of the
violence,
I've inflicted and endured
maybe thats the reason I've never been so self
assured.

Confidence in yourself is the biggest gift your family
gives you,
makes everything in life seem like less of an issue,
opens doors you didn't know you had to get through,
'cause the biggest demons you can face are stuck
there within you.

I've always had difficulty opening up,
always seemed to struggle to seem to give a fuck,
and sometimes my weakness is getting myself
to shutup,

'cause when my thoughts start spinning
I need paper and pen,
if I don't have these tools
I'm known to use a friend,
fuck knows I have, fuck knows I've learned,
and I would say god knows but we're not on speaking
terms since the tables turned, and my heart yearned
for someone who could really listen
with genuine concern,
I've heard thats all it takes,
a conversation with a mate ,
can make you sit back straight,
and reevaluate your mind-state.

Instagram: @poet_pricey